SIN AND I

SIN AND I
-TRAVIS HUPP-

atmosphere press

© 2024 Travis Hupp

Published by Atmosphere Press

Cover design by Josep Lledo

No part of this book may be reproduced without permission from the author except in brief quotations and in reviews.

Atmospherepress.com

AUTHOR'S NOTE

*"Be not conformed to this world: but be ye transformed
by the renewing of your mind"*
−Romans 12: 2

That passage from the Holy Bible is central to my work in this collection. As far back as I can remember, I've wondered what use God has for blind conformity. It's blind conformity that led to the Holocaust, after all. Blind conformity that led to every single one of Matthew Shepherd's murderers taking part in beating the tied-up young gay man to death. Blind conformity that led to silence from the Catholic church for so long in the face of horrendous child abuse. Blind conformity that led to racist violence against the very idea of equality in Charlottesville. Blind conformity that caused other police officers on the scene to do not much else but stand there idly for almost 10 minutes while George Floyd was slowly, painfully and publicly murdered by their colleague. Blind conformity has led to so many great evils throughout humanity's history, and only the refusal to conform *to* blind conformity has ever halted evil in its tracks.

The perception that Christianity champions conformity and the idea that anyone who questions it, or worse yet, acts against it, will burn in hellfire for eternity chased me away from organized religion for over 20 years. It can't be seriously argued that Christianity, as a whole, hasn't earned that perception. However, I've come to realize in the last few years that the last thing that will ever change that reality is for all the non-conformists to flee the religion.

Returning to Christianity as a gay man unashamed of myself for seeing the beauty of my own gender (just as God made me to) inspired poetry that I never could have written at any time in my life before now. Poetry that not only shines the disinfectant of sunlight on what conformists should be ashamed of, but tries to unflinchingly admit the sins that I *am* ashamed of committing myself. Even *(especially)* when the sin I'm repentant for lies somewhere else than where the conformist bigots who call themselves Christians think it is. Many times the biggest sin we can commit is to believe that something is sinful because we've been told it is, when not doing it (or, more accurately, pretending not to *be* it) is what feels more sinful to us. Many Christians bemoan others who believe that God exists, yet act as if He does not. Well, what could deny God's existence more than ignoring what He says to us as individuals because someone has cherry-picked something from the faith to say that God abhors it?

I will confess here and now that there have been times I acted as if God didn't exist, though I know He does. And every single time that occurred, it wasn't because I did something even though someone could point to passages of the Bible that can be construed to teach against it. Every single time, it was because I ignored that quiet but unmistakable voice within myself that I should have recognized as God guiding me along the path He intends for me, specifically, to walk.

Sin and I is about my repentance for the years I spent putting the sin of pretending not to hear God's voice ahead of living the truth God created me to live (to the point that God gave me a psychic awakening to prevent me from being able to ignore divinity, which I write about in my poetry). Now it's up to me to sort the signal from the noise and listen to what I believe God wants for, and *from* me.

It's my sincere hope that I've created something here that will speak to anyone, whether you're Christian or not. Whether you're gay, straight, bisexual, transexual, asexual, pansexual, non-binary or someone who is still doing the beautiful, necessary work of finding out who you are. No matter how many people have lied to you, telling you that God doesn't love you for being exactly who and what you are, right now, all you should need to enjoy this book is that instinctive, gut-level revulsion that comes from anyone ever trying to force you to live by so-called "values" that create, enable or rationalize oppression.

TABLE OF CONTENTS

- ANGER -

SELF DEFENSE	3
NON-ENTITY	4
OPEN AIR	7
COULDN'T (STILL CAN'T)	8
WRONG WRONG WRONG	
(a response to being gaslit)	9
BRAINS MELT	12
THE STRUGGLE'S STILL REAL	13
PERFECT WORD	15

- POLITICS -

DENSITY	19
LOOKING FOR MAGIC	20
SOMEONE YOU SHOULDN'T	23
MAKING LIGHT	25
HUNGER UNDER COVER	27
PUBLIC RECORD	30
AWARE	31
FOR FEAR	32
ALWAYS WITHIN US	33
STRONGHOLDS	34
THROWING BONES	35

- METAPHYSICAL -

NEVER OVER	41
A HIGHER PURPOSE	42
BY NOW BELOVED	45
TRIP WITH ME	47
NEXT LEVEL	48
TAPESTRY	49
GOOD THING	51
TRANSITORY STATE	52
SIN AND I	53

THE TRAP	54
FAITH CHANGES SHAPES	56
CENTURIES	58
BECKON	59
AWAITING ANSWERS	60
POSSESSED	61
WANDER OFF	62
GHOSTS	64
THAT'S WHY	65
GOD'S CREATION	66
GIMME BOTH, GIMME MORE	68
IN THE THROES	70
WAVELENGTHS	71

- DESPAIR -

RESILIENCE	75
STUPID FALLING STAR	76
DAYS OF BANISHMENT	78
EARLY LEAVE	79
TOP STORY	80
SPINNING TIRES	81
GENTLE HINT	82
THE SAME IN THE DARK	83
TROUBLED	84
GUNMETAL	85
READING SIGNS	86
VIGIL	87
BOGUS CHARGES	88
SPENT	89

- HOPE -

HEART OF A CITY	93
EMBEDDED	94
FEELING BETTER	96
SUBCONSCIOUS CAPACITIES	97
THINGS YOU CAN'T HAVE	98
GREY MATTER	99

FRIENDLIEST DEMON	100
JACKALS ATTRACTED	102
IT HURTS	103
MURDEROUS	104
TO REACH YOU	105
GEMEINSCHAFT	106
IF	107
SORROW'S SONG	109
PLANTING SEEDS IN A WARZONE	110
STRAY SPARK	111

- LOVE -

LOVELESS	115
ANTE UP	117
LET'S NOT FIGHT	118
KNOW THE DIFFERENCE	119
YOUR POWER	120
PLAY ON	121
NARROW ESCAPES	123
PAST MATTERING	125
TRUE TO MYSELF	126
WE LINGERED	128
LOVE'S UNLIMITED FORM	129
TRADING	130
NIGHTMARES OF YOU	131
VESSEL	132
REMINDING US	133
LOVE SONGS PROMISE NOTHING	134
WAYS TO BLEED	135
ANOTHER SPIN	138
HAIKUS ABOUT BEING AT YOUR MERCY	140
COSMIC FEVER	142
ALL OF THE ABOVE	143
GRAVITY	145
LOVE THEM AND ADMIT IT	146
THIS NEED	147
PRECIPICE (In memory of Oz, 2007 – 2023)	149

SELF DEFENSE

Wind off the mountains kicking up a fuss in the valley
Doing what I must with who I must
Nothing but downtime these days in the madhouse
The world's unjust and there's no one I trust
Voices are just noises chasing me outside from inside
Men devolving as loud as they can
Compulsory heterosexuality has me considering homicide
Shutting their mouths is really self defense
A place can catch fire for all kinds of reasons
Doing what I must to who I must
No one else here knows my personal demons
Which breed of monster am I forced to trust

NON-ENTITY

Immolate, lose all cohesion
Find someone frail and fragile to frighten
I don't scare easy, that's always been you
If I don't move you I might as well just walk through

You're ultimately insubstantial, there's just not much to you
You dither and dick around, you drown your own development
If you might further a worthy cause, instead you take a pause
between breaths, the sun sets, and your wind still ain't caught

Catch a tailwind out of my head
before you face plant in the trap you set

I hear your mouth running, it's just some dull buzzing
Your slang don't impress, your heart's a cold mess

Not even trying to warm over anything
the normals might find challenging

Are you anywhere at all, are you anyone you claim
You whisper and duck down before anyone registers your shade
Even if you signed it, you don't go by your name

Holster your hate so you can shoulder your share of blame
Berating my behavior while you act much the same
If it gets you irate, no one asked you to stay
Go find another closet, redo the whole cliché

You misread me and the situation
Your position's strength and the terrain

You made yourself something that fades
when you decided to just be pain

Acting like you won something 'cos you hurt me a little
For you, a little grief is all giving up takes
If it isn't easy, your tantrum takes up days
My bad, I'm a grown ass man, I didn't know
you still like games

Which means you can't be serious
Which means I can't be sidetracked
anymore into being bored while
we both pretend we think you're badass

I used to think a lot of you, now I think a little
I hate seeing you in such a state but
I can't post up in the middle
of your girlfriend and your ghost
and your gutless, gunless gangbanging
You're my groupies even though I refuse to perform
I'm not worried you'll move against me

I don't want what you assume I do
I'm neither limited nor captive
I won't limp with you through the same conversations
about things you say you're not, even though
it's you who brings up all of them

If you're not about it, stop talking about it
Instead of going on the attack, why not learn tact

You don't wanna grow up, so you try to cut me down
but you forget how long I've been around

Behind the blank wall you maintain in your mind
are aisles of agendas, racks of hats for every act
You have no idea how lucky you are
that it's hard to make me mad

No, I'm not chasing you down
Only in poetry will I react
My reason won't let me retaliate
just because I think it's sad

But I don't gotta keep doing this, either
I've revoked your privilege to let yourself in

You're neither ally nor enemy, you empty non-entity
Just some scrawny excuse that's wearing real thin

OPEN AIR

The state of fear where you live

The deepest deceit, trust you to love

The slur hurled at me fits you

Bad blood's drawn red but courses blue

Who knows what changes open air brings

Could that be why you're hiding things

What you're not saying is a clue

COULDN'T (STILL CAN'T)

Learned young.
This world?
Kill or be killed.
Truth thinly veiled.
Couldn't (still can't)
cut it much being cutthroat.
Cut my teeth on written words.
Gained citizenship in written worlds.
Dared not dabble in anything drawn.
Should've sensed somehow
weapons can be written.
Could I have known it?
Maybe so
but I didn't.
Couldn't fight rage off.
I can shape it
but only briefly escape it.

WRONG WRONG WRONG
(a response to being gaslit)

Voices from the sticks and brambles
looping feedback out their mouths
by way of their assholes
They cherry-pick my past
to support a narrative that collapses
Without revealing their qualifications
to diagnose me
or which of their own sins
became the devil
in their own recurring nightmares
It's all my fault they puff
I did it to myself
but it's them who really suffers
and who decides if I've suffered enough
I brought gifts to the table
I left them on the doorstep
It was wrong of me to do so
and wrong of me to stop it
I said too much of everything
in places where people
say anything to say nothing
I'm stubborn and slow to learn
they proclaim stubbornly
ad nauseum
They follow me everywhere
insisting I'm going nowhere
They blame me for everything
while insisting I'm capable of nothing
I said it wrong

I did it wrong
I woke wrong
Slept wrong
Ate wrong
Walked wrong
Was gone too long
Overstayed my welcome wantonly
Welcomed weirdos way too warmly
Gave up too easy because I
couldn't keep the faith
Which doesn't contradict
calling me gullible
in a single fucking way
If I just got over my trust issues
I'd know why trust will get you played
Until I internalize their incessant insight
I'm wrong about anything I might write
Anything I didn't write or
might consider writing instead
It's wrong
Just wrong
So wrong wrong wrong
because the source of it all is someone
so fundamentally incorrect
Incorrect yet also too innocent
Naturally I was involved in no intrigue
before their invasion
when they plunked down
their intractable asses
to grace me endlessly
with their attention
without which I'd never existed yet

Now I exist as their shameful secret
who can never say anything of note
but always needs to say less
The two things they say
I must know for sure
is they know I'm hiding something
and they're lying
If I could
I'd be hiding all of me
Until they stop finding me
I'll keep trying

BRAINS MELT

Keep it up then, go on applying for the position
of my monologuing nemesis
when I wasn't even hiring

So sick of being stricken by plots that don't thicken
Slackjawed from standing by while you suck sense itself
into your singularity

You feel called upon to clarify

Into a black hole swirls clarity

Is your destiny to drain me
Instead you're draining everything

Infinity's still inexhaustible, right?
Surely the science on that is sturdy

Brains melt before your bullheadedness, outmatched
Your nihilism never notices corners
exist to keep me trapped

Other than nothing, only winning and losing
Seems important to your belief system
Always snatching at some stupid prize

The meaningless void and its champion

THE STRUGGLE'S STILL REAL

After so much has been said
what more is there to say
Should I say nothing or maybe rephrase

The harrowing hurt that grows worse
no matter what it teaches me

The prized passion glitching and guttering
before it ever reaches me

The latest update is that
the struggle's still real
I only make the best of it
because there's no better deal

I can be aggressively antisocial
unsparingly judgmental in my thoughts
I don't tell that to people often
because I don't like talking to twats

Maybe if more people acted
like they knew how to walk through doors
without holding them shut on
the person behind them
my demeanor would be less sore

But then there are the trickier times
when I'm inexplicably
overcome with sentiment
Romanticizing interactions
inflating what they meant

Maybe they would mean something
if more people noticed the quicker kindnesses
and then I wouldn't always feel
woefully short of alliances

After absorbing insults
and hurling them back
Should I eat crow or reinforce my attack

It's hell to strut impaled
by the blade on which you fell

Especially after sharpening it first
but dull apologies rarely sell

So the latest update is that
the struggle still kills
As for saying sorry or standing firm
I guess this is how I feel

Fuck every truth I've told
By further suffering rewarded
Yet also fuck the liars
and the riches laid before them

PERFECT WORD

Holy fuck I'd do so much
if lifted by the wind I lost

If I had a clue of the cure
to what I don't know I'm inured

If I could excavate the perfect word

If my will never wobbled
If my hand stayed steady
If my presence of mind
wasn't company property

If peace was a part of me left
after every automatically deducted percentage

If saying "enough" was ever easy
If we learned each other's lessons

DENSITY

They'll try to make you think
a density of lies
is a complexity of lies

But no
It's just dense
It's not deep
So it makes no sense
to lose anymore sleep

LOOKING FOR MAGIC

And still I'm looking for magic outgrown
When I had it I was too young
to be wise about its use
I just invented unlikely characters to talk to
Doomed action figures to gory death
at interstellar war
Shaded by an oak in my back yard
Now the dreams
The monuments
For that which I think was
back when I feared reprisal enough
to say it was not
I can only imagine what the invented say
to some other grubby child
Melted Dr. Crusher and shish kabobbed Thundercats
Screaming "OH MY GOD WE CONCEDE DEFEAT!"

But inevitably, he or she
Will be course corrected by starchy authority:
The moment you clear five feet, things are your responsibility. Meaning prioritize what's been valued by generations before you. It doesn't matter why, just get hired for a job you'll despise. Like expected, you'll be straight. Like mercury, find a bride. If you're uncertain about your future together, it usually helps to have a child. It might seem like most families are all kinds of insane, but all the same, carry forward the name.

Such muted magic in the masses
Shuffling dutifully through drudgery
Shirking what their spirit's saying
'cos Princess Portly is getting mad at Tastee Freez
where the workers get 12 bucks an hour
and still don't seem to care that she

wants that milkshake *now*
But instead, the indignity of a two minute wait
all because a prospective ice cream dispenser
was fucking around writing poems all day
Most of us will cave
Most of us will hate it
Stretch our dismay across our faces
in convincing smiles til we can't take it
Putting peanuts aside from each paycheck
for a budget friendly escape

It's just how life is, the franchise manager will proclaim
We pay so we can work and we work so we can pay:
This is how we do things here. This is all we do here. Sweep the floor faster with more obvious pride or get a verbal warning before you're swept aside. We'll tell you what to say. We'll pull your cord and you'll say it. Unless the customer specifically asks for the truth, never over explain it. When you work retail you better check your conscience at the door. It's the customer's idiot fault if they don't know this is war.

Unreliable magic in assembly line matrimony
Making love a matter for lawyers
Joining two people by the power of God
who the paperwork says has a job at the local circuit court
If I tell someone I love them
If they believe me and reciprocate
Every day we find ways to be wed
Ceremony that never needs to be done
once we've begun
Minus red tape to restrict our movement
If we feel it ending and need to move on

How can we know abiding love will carry us through all our days
Without the reinforcement of an accountant reading off
our list of tax breaks?:
For richer or poorer, meaning 50/50 odds we end up suing each other.
Forsaking all others except the government whose permission must be
attained before we even consider running away.

I keep missing the magic
Inherent in simplicity
I've decided to just stop looking
so the magic can find me

SOMEONE YOU SHOULDN'T

Are you getting caught loving and lusting again
Do you love someone you shouldn't
Do you have a plan A
Or B through Z
Or will you wing it

Will you wing it or will you skip it
What feathers will you ruffle
What pyrrhic victory will you wring of all meaning
Is there an attic or a basement
to provide privacy for your keening
Somewhere you figure no one can hear you
but they probably could if they chose to

Face forward, eyes darting around
Fugitives just can't be forthcoming
in every day situations
Never be the first to confess anything
or you'll be abandoned to your punishment

Fantasy is reality's punishment
but at least we have our limited freedom
You can lie and pine wherever you please
within reason
You can hate your life in a sun dappled park
or a bus terminal in the dark

You can go without at work
or at Walmart
or in your room

You can have nothing everywhere
in this land of opportunity
Why aren't you gelling with the jingoism
Why isn't your smile sterling
A real man's grin never loses its sorrow proofing
A guy too sad to shovel shit is just a brat

Why can't you take it like a man
who isn't there
and be resigned to that?

MAKING LIGHT

Making light of every issue makes things murky and encourages foolishness

We are a selfish species, inexcusably ill-informed

Fundamentally unqualified to know what's best for us

We keep deciding it's war for all

War against ourselves, against our neighbors

War for the motherland and founding fathers

to fuck over foreigners

Shredding evil evidence, subjugating what's sacred

So vain in our virtue it becomes our vice

Getting high to feel alive when we die

Rest brings recriminations, we're on our feet and sleeping

We're too catatonic to vet our journalists so we just complain that there's no difference

There are many, we just don't know

Ready your fact sheet with its bullet points

but we don't want to be shown

It's so fucking funny isn't it

Ignorance of injustice is so good for comedy

At least we'll sit beside each other to laugh a while

about every pillar that props us up toppling

HUNGER UNDER COVER

Awake because the weather's weird in my head
Spirits moving me toward paradigm shift
Caterwauling worries, capitalism needs cash
Body led in my bed, mind on more than germy trash

Night birds aren't singing, I wonder why not
I'm heavy to lift tonight but the moon pulls me up
and out to see if the stars are still where they should be
Humans give this planet hell, the natural world is collapsing

Suppose I'll start writing since I suck so hard at sleep
or find a country boy on Grindr who claims he's straight
Make believe that's my fetish, make a show of taking him serious
Men around here will give their ass up, but if you call them gay,
they're furious

Energy ebbs, the menu's bare bones
The dudes nearby last night are still the only ones close
No one new visiting the Airbnb next door
but a possum strewing garbage decoratively across the porch

He's charmingly ugly, or I guess maybe "she"
Hunger under cover of night is equal opportunity
Hope whatever scent summoned them tastes their
version of decadent
Told God I'd be in church tomorrow but by
then I'll be convalescent

My cycle doesn't sync, I'm awake when nothing's happening
or asleep when an obligation can be scandalized by my absence
I'll miss the sermon, then the matinee with that
really nice guy it'll never work with

But some of us, it seems, must tilt up at the sky
Confirming our stars, ogling marsupials like spies
Hating that money matters, mad restless to make it not
Notching every evening since we blew our last best shot

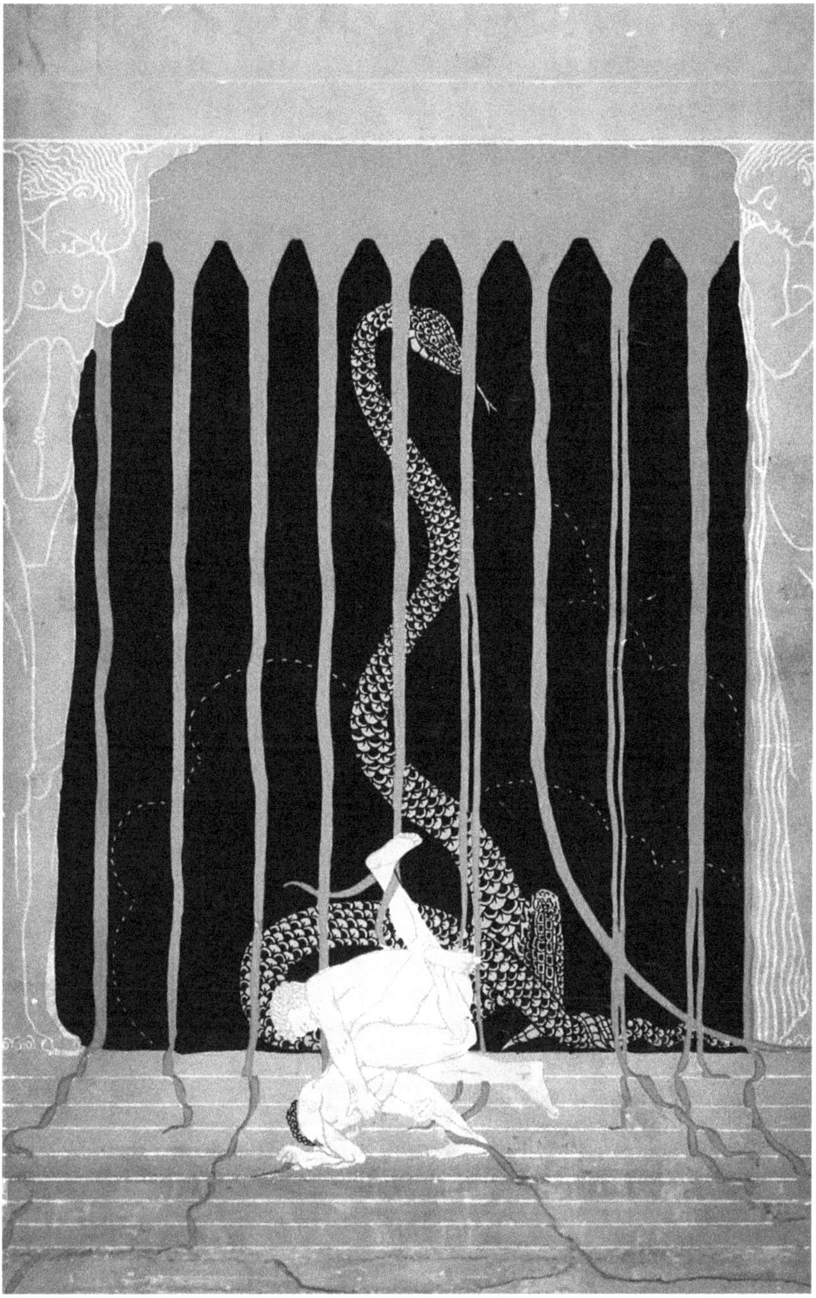

PUBLIC RECORD

Looking on the bright side, fighting on the right side

The right side is the left side, the left side is the pride side

I give better than I get 'cos I ain't got nothing yet

It's no reason to fret, I set my heart on the best bet

The best bet is highly unlikely, not every day mundanity

Oh my God, the humanity, what's normal is just insanity

Who are we without each other, my badass brother lover

If our secrets weren't public record, we could keep that under cover

AWARE

I'm aware what I am
isn't quite what you are
You're aware what will be said
if you're near more often than far

If I'm the one who calls you "faggot" first
will you stick with me
instead of those jerks?

FOR FEAR

All it takes is one
with ignorance implacable
and an onlooking throng
that won't defend
anyone gay
for fear of the rumor mill

ALWAYS WITHIN US

Everyone we could be is always within us
Who are you now, who do you disavow
You either decide or it's decided for you
Is there any pleasure or treasure you're not allowed

Who are you now, who do you disavow
Your disparate selves or your desperate detractors
Is there any pleasure or treasure you're not allowed
Make your move now and think about it after

Your disparate selves or your desperate detractors
Someone defines you for the world even if you
can't be bothered with it
Make your move now and think about it after
Don't leap hurdles set up for you, just go around that shit

Someone defines you for the world even if you
can't be bothered with it
You can use their misconception and leave them to stew in it
Don't leap hurdles set up for you, just go around that shit
You know your rights, what's the law got to do with it

STRONGHOLDS

The normal, whiny cacophony any time anyone speaks against heteronormativity. I'm not gonna stop noticing the glint of important points straight people purposely miss. I won't say sorry because I said something else instead of the lazy lines the normals are fed. Sometimes the counterculture's just gotta represent.

The uproar is endless and inane. No matter how much you keep the trauma contained, someone will tell you to clutch it quieter. Someone who might be worth something as a witness won't want the responsibility of knowing better. Of being wiser.

I've had guys threaten me one on one and five at a time. If people wanting me dead was fatal I guess I would've died. I remain stubbornly alive to spit spite in their eyes. We owe oppressors nothing, the oppressors will know what we're owed. We must go freely among them, strong enough to crumble their strongholds.

THROWING BONES

Silence might kind of sting now
The forest and I had a fight
Now the birds are cold shouldering me
and the bugs are getting in my eyes

The neighbors are restless
if those are the neighbors tromping about
Trampling my focus
Amazed by everything, interminably loud

I'll crank my volume up too then
Roar my poetry til it shakes down some leaves
"Delighted to meet everybody" I'll boom
"It's not exhausting at all, feeling everything
so deeply"

"If you really listen to the way the verses interplay
I think you'll find the message is clearly
go away"

I guess they never get it, because they stay
Sure, art's subjective, but it isn't today

I have a clear point in my line of sight
Something profound like "most people mostly lie"

I have no idea if that's true, which
reinforces my thesis
but I'm struck with surly sentiments
that keep away transcendence

What gangly monster am I writing here
and what does it need to accomplish

It's never for nothing, what waits to emerge til now
Something important tends to eventually spill out

Important to poets, anyway
Who walk around pondering big questions like
"Do onions know?"

It's still hard to believe such investigations can earn a living
but I've seen the proof they can earn a subsisting

Most art is starved by capitalism
'til it can only be known by throwing bones

If I won't say that's ok, does that tacitly
condone the insurrection
Could it possibly even matter
Poetry's lost on redneck petulance

I am lost and not entirely loathing it
I find fragments of fulfillment in fits
Count the rings of a hundred trees
hacked down in a killing spree
to clear some clean air
out of the way of humanity

Like any invasive species
we massacre what we please
Make homes of our stolen habitats
So comfy and pretty
The dead and displaced
just manifest destiny

We stroll by souls slumped in streets
Spare them snack money, barely
Take pity rarely

It's all so vibrant and fatal
Such deprivation drowned out
by so much first world festivity
Sickening smog, choking our therapy dogs

The clash of cussing crazies and catcalling carnies

So many points lose their edge
So many meanings get mulled over
and spooled out well past their mark

Teenage folly distracts me, kids bragging too big for their britches
Trashing the traphouse across from the park
Blaring songs full of slurs, a little light on heart

Is youth no longer a synonym for idealism
I try to detect some social conscience
and I'm traumatized by a twerking trainwreck

I don't know for sure every substance they're on
But they're so wide open they're like a meal for cops

It presents a dim view as the day falls to dark
I regard them over my notebook, seeking some substance
In their rebellion's spark

But these kids won't fight conformity
They seem like the type to fight to conform

Same swagger, same style, depressingly uniform

My disappointment is unreasonable, unfathomable
Sudden rain slashes at me sharply
Like God caught me judging, so I caught the storm

I lurch away from lances of lightning
Run rumpled through the downpour
Admonished by my Lord

METAPHYSICAL

NEVER OVER

I kind of want to stay sober

or maybe a buzz that's never over

I gotta balance so many varied angles

to finally sort my devils from angels

The uncanny inkling I can't ignore is

They'd rather get sordid than get sorted

Eternal villain and the virtue ever courted

A HIGHER PURPOSE

Start with some preamble previewing
new thematic material
Then go out and find it
Fresh fights, new sources of light
Something other than my history
repeating itself

A higher purpose glimpsed
Clouds that thin and dissipate

A cat that stays 'cos he's not
the scaredy kind
instead of skipping out
when he only just skipped in

A man who acts like he wants to win
but knows "winning", in this life,
just means not losing
At least not everything
At least not always

Last gasp muffled
Salvation snatched
The planet keeps moving

So does every other planet
Some say other worlds seeded Earth
Ancient aliens, some folks go all in on that
Is there a polite way to ask them
if they're the bozos who think it's flat

Could God be even less limited
in form and flight than I figured
Maybe he outsourced creating us
Sent basic instructions with
a foldout of helpful pictures

Maybe the stuff of us needed to be
coaxed into coalescing
by an absurd primordial space opera
of invaluable elements and sheisters
stealing from each other
back and forth, from universe to universe
Cross pollinating, correctly
these random mcguffins
'til finally, there we were
Hungry and horny and wearing nothing

For a time, fucking and eating was our higher purpose
For a time, for some, it still is
For some, even hedonism has
components of spirit

But nothing negates the summons
to do good work forever
For those whose spiritualism holds
hedonistic components
For whom, a worthy job is a pleasure

Components, bleeding together recklessly,
from moment to
predestined moment
Some of this, a generosity of that
Merged with a wish of a

sweet son who snapped

Then clambered back
Then broke deeper
Put myself under such pressure
until I remembered

In the final analysis, it's all just
thematic material
We are all thematic material
Flesh wrapped around the ethereal

BY NOW BELOVED

Some of what I hear I can imagine myself imagining

Some other parts, I can't imagine why I'd imagine that

The phantoms claim I created them to provide me
quality case management

The part of me cut off from everything brings skepticism to bat

Sometimes deep bass voices rumble their list of demands

Sometimes tentative whispers invite me to ignore my own senses

The bullies talk just right, make getting roughed up
seem so attractive

The infantry sends word to the cavalry, inventories defenses

Some of what I see is a vision inside, hijacking
my mind's eye

Some other sights are right before me where I hide, swooping
from troubled skies

The former is equally easy to deny or to embrace

The latter can't be debunked, they tempt fate wearing an
appealing face

Sometimes I rifle off clever retorts or brag about
my faith's strength

Sometimes I buckle and bargain, swear I'll obey if they
just go away

The reality I'm realizing is so uncomfortable I haven't until
now admitted it

The unreality is by now beloved, if it left I'd
scramble after it

TRIP WITH ME

Road trip with me and my playlist
about road trips for the drive
We'll pick up every hitchhiker
'cos we know what walking's like
How your legs go numb beneath you
How you lose all sense of time

And if there's something impossible crouched just ahead
blending in with an oily night
or there are demons flitting between trees
flanking the road on both sides
Well you'd have to rely on your wits
and whatever sad weapon
concealed in your pocket
Just to get back to your street
which you've always known is haunted

NEXT LEVEL

What I felt was some
next level shit
Grinding jaws and instruments
Soundtrack for a trip
I wrote it in the dust
that swirled in your wake
and spiraled down on me
so I could
take it to my grave

TAPESTRY

Hidden threads
weave and unfurl me
obscuring the potential
for nirvana sewn into me
Crafted meticulously

Stitching a truth
that often eludes me
That I've been tearing
since cognizance dawned on me
Closest approximation
of recovery
is admitting
I'll forever be torn

While all this life
it swirls around me
In breezes
In gales
In waves that deluge me

Slow drag of quicksand
Just enough purchase
in mysterious purpose
to briefly
halt my sinking

So I gather data
Make deductions
Reconfigure riddles
in my skull
where they're clinging
Sensing all the while
the confusion is
as it should be

Paradox
embodied in flesh
Part of a grander tapestry
A tapestry bright
Connected but torn
Shredded and born
Isolated entities

GOOD THING

People try to block me
Everyone together stops me

I'm alone and surrounded
broken apart by sirens sounding

I say God first
and no one knows who I mean

I say you first
and no one thinks the next step is safe

I say me last
and everyone seems to agree

Good thing I believe in eternity

TRANSITORY STATE

Click on my flashlight
Spotlight conversations
Nugs and blunts and crystals
cast the shadow wasteland

Not addicted so much as attached to
this transitory state
Smoke keeps the spotlight otherwise engaged

A ring of truth in an arid room, barely ringing
Generation of deficits
For example: attention, excuses

Debauchery straddles both sides of
my bittersweet New Year's eve
I can feel the optimistic promise I'm drunk on
aging out of its power by the hour

I tell myself I've felled isolation, that I've learned
to detect the undetectable, rippling a pond
See the glare off the surface instead of
the surface itself
That I'm as ready as I've ever been
to do good work, to work hard
To be a sibling to anyone harmed

SIN AND I

God says have faith in His son

The cards say hurt and move on

Logic says don't count on the sun

Odds say I'm due to face a gun

No one alleges I'll find the one

No one hits me up for fun

Sin and I had quite a run

THE TRAP

One man battalion
Standard grade bombardment

Of energies pulsing
Of puerile insults that nearly make sense

Now you're curious, conversing
how long past midnight, with
what revenant?

Just like that, the trap is set

All Hell, was it you said? What of Avalon?
Whose sundry strategy? Who inherits whose debts?

Past and present tense arcing away on
wings of darkness
All at once, all syllables sound
A wall of words, I just can't parse it

Except, as they glide for skies far and away
they circle overhead to caw in unison
"You'll pay, oh yes, you'll pay"

What manner of tribute could I have
paid in days hence?
What ill-gotten bling did I bring
under dark hypnosis?

All words encompassed, every one rendered dubious
Abstract nouns are slithering around, led by voyeurism
Spite is here, turning curiosity to jealousy and suffocation
Sex is here, saying "Look!". Screaming "letch!".
Sighing "none for you!"
Despondence dumbs me down. Fastidiousness
finds some screws loose.
Gluttony, so good to me, if we're goners let's eat everything

Chewing the scenery, it's chewing us back
Devouring everywhere right off the map

FAITH CHANGES SHAPES

Shadows descend, shatter me again

Even after some questions found answers

Got me re-evaluating my definition of enlightenment

Because I have learned

I've grown, I've drawn conclusions

None of which prevents my loneliness

When I'm unrequited and benighted

My faith changes shapes, I try to keep up

With what it is and isn't

What it will be and was

What it might be

What it costs me

What it will abide and won't

'til the mixture overflows

with volatility exposed

Simple to advocate fearlessness, harder to enact it

when your imagination is so much dynamite

and your fuses perpetually tampered with

Yet I do believe in the best of me

to find some love for even the worst

I'm an addict locked in conflict

confident in my competence to purge myself pure

I have a bitter streak, acidic in me

and presence of mind to keep it in check

A mouth that runs away with me

and a heart that means no disrespect

Shadows obscure, as is the nature of shadows

Mostly, I've decided enlightenment

is sparking your mind to dispel darkness

When loneliness is your only company

Loneliness must speak

CENTURIES

There is the elusive feeling
of centuries
locked away in grey matter
The obtrusive feeling
of remembering
too often to ignore

If ever I truly remembered
I'd live life
a shambling fracture
So I'm careful
what I wish for
Though careless
what I pursue

BECKON

Dividing and dividing
each into cells (in all the word's meanings)
Shouting over walls while bricking them higher

Divided, you against me
Me against a simplistic reading of reality

My fault who I was but
I splintered him off me
Broke him into shards and snide barbs
against the walls and floors and
ceilings of identity

The vanishing voices keep returning
A poem that was singular
Dividing
Keeps dividing

An army of agitation unleashed
Who summoned who with what beckon?

What wretched aspect runs me down to reckon?

AWAITING ANSWERS

Is my trauma due to being in love?

Am I confusing "in love" with "butchered and hung"?

Does electricity power me?

Does God?

Is God electricity?

Can God fall in love?

Does it hurt when God smiles?

When God's butchered and hung?

How can God know us yet forgive all we've done?

POSSESSED

Falsely friendly, manic as meth
I'm just pissed the demon thinks
I'm the one possessed

Dreams might come true, just a little deranged
That's all I'll
offer this ragamuffin fiend

who someone dropped off
deluded into thinking
it could take one cell of me

Bitch will curtsy and be polite,
I tell it,
Bitch always says thank you and please

WANDER OFF

Somewhere out there are infinite
branches of reality
forming dimensions where I get
screwed over completely differently

Where I run the wrong guy off
instead of letting him stay
Where I wander off a curb
without glancing either way

Where I hold my peace
and run my mouth
in opposite instances
pursue unlikelihoods to
different distances

Where I stop writing
after middle school
or never even begin
Fall out of love with
my lonely hobbies
Where I pick up a gun instead of a pen

Where I keep far better records
of the order in which
who played who for a fool

Where I entertain all different folly
Only go to jail for things I do

Somewhere, a me aborted
or a me who dies young and memorably
A me who dies gnarled and forgotten
hoping he helped anyone with anything

Infinite permutations of
one in a billion hapless dudes
Happier than his circumstances suggest
Tripping after abundant truth

GHOSTS

Day and night they tear me apart
Night and day I repair my heart
Who they seek to destroy for who
I'm not sure but there are clues
What to do but just give in
Let ghosts decide what's right or sin
I might lose but they won't win

In fight or flight they build me up
All our mood swings are so abrupt
Pieces of me or people even stranger
More in peril when I feel safer
Are we at odds, are we friends
Are we both, all at wits end
The tactile world is what feels pretend

THAT'S WHY

Our forgiveness for the world
is a wonder when unfurled
The world wants to see it
That's why it kicks our teeth in

GOD'S CREATION

Storms are God's creation
purifying pummeling
We hunker where we need to
Weather Channel isn't foolproof
Few things ever are but
there's another world that's ours
A clearing of debt for a promise kept

Let's hold up our side
Heaven, let's try

Prayer while fasting
Voice of spirits undelineated
People sent to each other, surely
for something more than
hedging our bets

I answered your knock
Let you in from the elements
You still haven't said what
storm chased you to my step

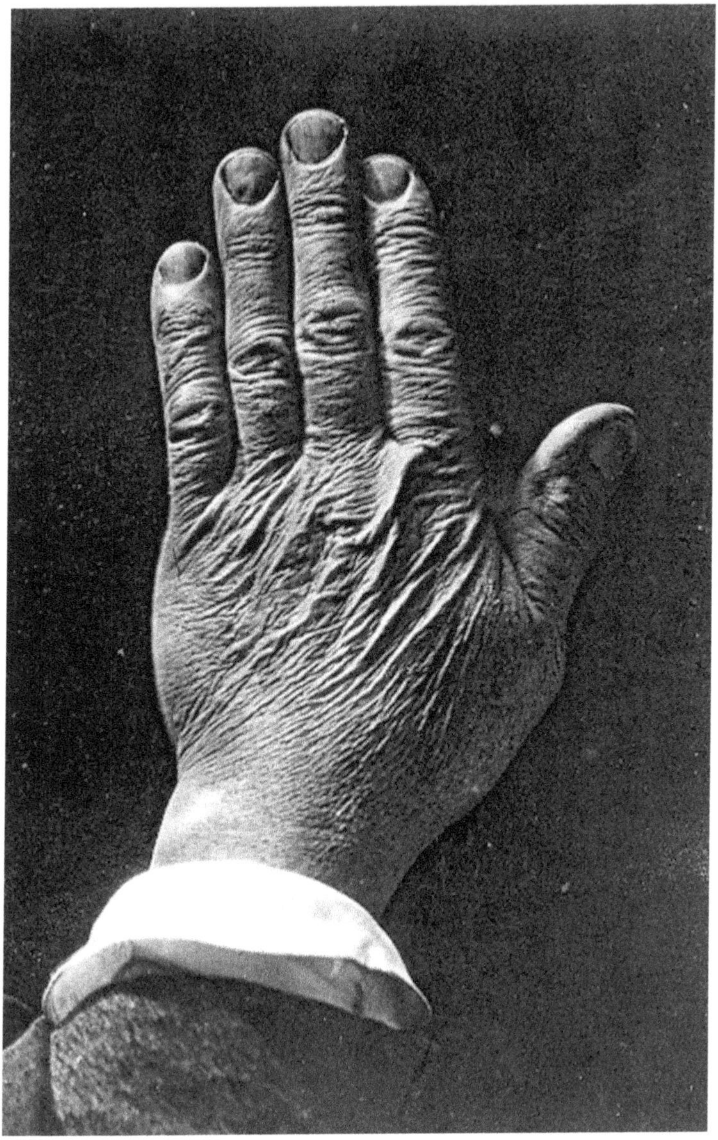

GIMME BOTH, GIMME MORE

Around and around, down and down
Psi-war ensues, word gets out
Invisible vigils, crowded heads
Erstwhile family, bad neighbors now instead

Manifestations of loneliness, creature comfort cure alls
Kept calling him the wrong name, now he's got me by the balls

What I hear is real, entirely intact illusions
Why do I fear what I feel, why never one clean conclusion

Back to back, face to face
A game of grab-ass in a garden of grace
Nightly intruders ingratiate themselves endlessly
A man I think beautiful liars incorporeal call unsightly
In hiding when they hit me, in case their own masks slip slightly

Rock and rap, my taste verses yours
My perspective evolves, gimme both, gimme more
Night terror, dream life, always sleeping wide awake
Benched a while, back in style, brave from blind faith

Third eye still sees, blunders still make bank
Overnight success in 42 years and a day
Hear them laughing, murmuring agreement
Hear them heckle 'til Hell hauls them off

A lot of assumptions, something for nothing
Learn their natures, breathe their vapors
Lay down cards, know the cost

Meaning ain't fleeting, flashbacks of feelings
I caught once catching up, I catch them and let them
Infuriating attitudes of casual dudes
One minute I'm proclaiming my politics and then
he hits his half-assed refrain and I'm captivated again

IN THE THROES

Don't let him catch you caring
Don't let him catch you alone
He'll leave you crumpled; thoroughly deboned

Pleasure's powerful pain, he'll discard you
moaning in the throes
Know when to let him go
The fantasy won't hold

Won't warm your cockles
Won't win your slobberknockers

When you're besieged; broken of belief

Faith's carnal crisis, feral phantoms
in attack formation beneath
Be loud enough to be found
by mercy's myriad beauty

Try something new
A favorite color after blue
A specific shade of weaponized rainbow
sparking off the chip on your shoulder

So sorry what smothered should have smoldered

WAVELENGTHS

Do you know
the wavelengths of your soul
The imprints you've been leaving
everywhere you go
That there are those of us
who can walk
where you walked
and never see you
Knowing just the same
that you have
recently been there

DESPAIR

RESILIENCE

My devoted family has been
certain of my improved fortunes for weeks
So convinced of my resilience are they
they don't bother checking to see

Passersby smile and wave
Ask how I'm doing
I say I'm alright

My friends assure me they're here for me
through static
via satellite

"Repeat what you just said" I say
"Somebody say something real"

"FootballpussyI'llfightyou" they say
Reassured is not how I feel

STUPID FALLING STAR

Instantaneous poetry.
Three words
Four syllables:

Life is lonely.

Is this genius yet?
What have decades
of freestyle beget?

Torturous, yes
but still I submit.
Flying blind more often
than I care to admit.

I don't know exactly
how I'm injured.
How I have been
all along.

Even the paths
most gilded
cast only iron thoughts.

The beseeching clang
of my steel
on empty plates
in a mess hall
where only I starve
while everyone else
makes easy meals
of every stupid
falling star.

Still they talk at me
Pretentious enough
to tell me what
hurts who
how much.

DAYS OF BANISHMENT

I will take with me the coiled apprehension
your vanishing instilled

Getting blitzed in a seedy motel
Five hours beyond midnight's tolling bell

This mutant love
transformed when rebuffed

I confess these powers were activated by experiments
I can still only fumble to focus clumsily through instruments

Tarot cards and Bible passages on shuffle
So appropriate it gets eerie

Sixth sense sharp as shards, bringing revelations
less than ravages in these days of banishment

You were always about to get near me
but my charms just raise your alarms

I'm marooned among savages
appraising all too many sadnesses

You must be some serious
metaphysical dart of poison

In fever dreams I mostly
make the same shaky choices

EARLY LEAVE

I make my half-assed excuses
to take my early leave
from the party's desperate
twelve hour blare

Same episode every week

TOP STORY

Tonight's top story:
PEOPLE ARE LOVING ANYWAY
Hoping all the same
Meeting for their tall and frothies
Polishing the grime
Handing out the Oscars
and other news agencies
are shilling other narratives
than ours, which goes:
IT'S FUCKING OVER
WE NEVER REALLY
DID OUR BEST
WE NEVER REALLY
WANTED TO

SPINNING TIRES

A head full of spinning tires and the smell of burning rubber fearful my past will find me or that I'll never find it semi-wishing I could have Alzheimer's and be whoever I still remember forgetting I lost my center and damn the night sky looks bright enough to sit outside and read by but I won't 'cos I'm a fool who thinks he has energy for anything without his medicine and my dreams are getting as bad and as violent as the news is and I don't know what I want anymore so I don't know how to get it but I know I don't want advice from perspectives I can't stomach 'cos I've exhausted any beauty I exaggerated in my sadness used up every alibi bled through every bandage smoked up every cigarette wanting to choke on every drag bitten every bullet bitten every hand that brought me plates of total bullshit lightly salted supposedly with tears but I don't believe they'd cry for me or ever cry at all 'cos they're too damn scared to feel and I wonder why I love them and why I'm so easy to abandon and I wish that I could hate them but I can't and I can't stand it and I could tell them that I'm tired but most wouldn't catch my meaning and I could tell them that they're vicious but of course they know already

GENTLE HINT

I've pried every mind
Fell through glass inside
and bled

Rickety
shaking structures
Shaken down
around each other
at a gentle
hint of wind

Can I afford to forgive
There are things
I need to live
I'm bombarded by
some crackpot analysis
every time I
cast a shadow

Pushed from room
to room by
the volatile expansion
of too many egos

The doors
already swallowed
I'm escaping by
a window

THE SAME IN THE DARK

You can't really suffer if you really don't care
That's why villains can't be punished and
heroes can't be spared

The person somewhere between
Unsure what the differences mean
Just languishes

Heroes and villains
abuse the same languages

They look the same in the dark
Patronize the same bars

Maybe it's best to lock yourself alone in your room
and battle the hero and villain in you

TROUBLED

Maybe I shouldn't bother
to worry, work or write
or listen to doctors
Maybe I shouldn't
nurture new ambitions
Just say my current state
is enough for me
but I'm coming up empty
and God knows I got needs

I am alone
I am troubled
because I'm not in love and
the wrong stories keep getting longer

GUNMETAL

The smoke is cashed quickly
Youth spent frivolously
Nights flicker by
Stars deceive our minds
Wishes drift Heavenward
Try and feel when they're heard
Makes us feel better
Smooths the ruffled feathers
'til we think we can fly again
but we limp to bed instead
Dreaming of adventure
Staying asleep forever
Warmed by blanket and steel
Our gunmetal doesn't know fear
Our trigger fingers never get itchy
We mean it when we aim it
We're not known for missing
We blaze away and sleep it off
Bleed our neighbors and walk our dogs
Just smile real wide
while we make people cry
Jack that self-esteem up
'til it can't fit under the sky
Plates and panoramas shifting
Unforgiving new terrain
We starve unless we yield
We're devoured unless we change
There's the sense that we should
have some say in the matter
and the thunder of a laughing God
A trace of race memory
from a time we stood by each other
Surefooted in purpose
before being made to crawl

READING SIGNS

Yes, I'm capable of reading signs, like

"Keep this door closed at all times"
"Think nothing of this, we're just playing"
"If anyone hears, you'll never stop paying"
"Don't read signals I send by mistake"
"Make me feel and I'll run away"

That's the state of gay pride today

VIGIL

Friction heated time, days run together
Snapshots of insomnia, pooling in puddles
To what end, I wonder
My stubborn, constant vigil
I deserve so much better, my spirit is willing

Well, I'm counting walls and taping up pictures
and finding some beauty, but it's hardly adventure

I could exist with just mind free, not body
Make my frame for taking aim before
my psyche goes sling-shotting
But being able to move with no movement here to join
and no one following my lead
is getting annoying

BOGUS CHARGES

Trust went bust, safety's a sham
I don't know who they think they are
thinking they know who I am

By my friends ghosted
By my latest mantra propped up
By God I'll catch schemers scheming
By then I'll have summoned my guts

Guess I gotta show guile for a while
Be conniving, love lying
Terrorized by trickery
Turning ideas around for turnabout
Authorities almost certainly in on it
Anyone I love even a little
probably secretly selling me out

My dreams tell on me, tell them everything
so they can trump up bogus charges
My allegiances subjected to heat lamp and microscope
Even pleasure is plausibly part of it
Bestowed just to bewitch me, I bet
Hands that caress me can also choke me

Assailed by the same souls I stood up for
For looking them in the eyes, will mine be blackened
Will they starve me mad when I'm mad already
I already feel the quicksand where
traitors unmasked will leave me stranded

SPENT

Closed mouths don't get fed, it's said
but I opened mine and emptied
all the sound in my head
and still I never have near enough bread

Still waiting on the cost/benefit analysis
of grievances already aired
'til I ran out of synonyms for "unfair"

Someone tell me
where they're sending my checks
If it's this dimension they
got my addy wrong

Here love's limited
Not where I'm goin'

HOPE

HEART OF A CITY

I guess this is it
I'm really doing it
Leaving; arriving
as I please; on my own schedule
in the heart of a city
whose heart is changing color
I, in my basement apartment,
will play my part
to influence the spectrum
But damn I start out feeble
Shaky and in the red
I still don't fully believe
I still can't fully forget
that I'm doing this alone now
By myself; for myself
That the city's heart
like any other's
may simply not accept me
That every foot set outside
might turn me right back in
That I don't know how
I've gone so long without
So I'm willing naked need to mean
the sprawl will supply my demands

EMBEDDED

No matter how many reasons
you give them to smile
some find reasons to hate

To glare, to demean
To demand explanations they've
no intention of understanding

No creative license can
put charm in their scorn
Fault must be found
They won't sit and hear a poem

They interrupt when they please
All damn day, all damn week
Interpret information through
some fucked up filter

Friends are to fight
Fighters long to be killers

They make noise about mapping
your moral compass
The hot air they heave is all filler

I kind of just want to
be kind to someone
who doesn't react like
a nice guy is a leper

Who doesn't forward my
every fetish
'til the skies
blare the message

Who won't disappear
the very moment
I count on them
Leaving me to tear out
the years embedded

FEELING BETTER

I'm realizing dreams these days,
I'm putting down my airs.

I'm not pretending I know everything,
or any significant portion thereof.

I'm steeling myself for loss, but hoping
just once life might be fair.

I'm not spending my good luck frivolously, or
going broke for drugs.

I'm feeling better every day, yet keeping
creation's cyclical movements in mind.

I'm not above feeling sorry for myself, but I
can feel glad for me too.

I'm reeling from the bad old days, yet appealing
to every good spirit I can find.

I'm not saying it's enough, that there aren't reasons to give
up, but what's finally true is none of them are you

SUBCONSCIOUS CAPACITIES

All I can do is more than I think

Everyone buries subconscious capacities

Wherever I am is more than surfaces under surfaces

I get hung up in strange places discerning what my own vested interest is

Opinions, unsolicited, disembodied, mouthless, lungless

Underfed, oversexed, disinterested in more disillusionment

So don't mind if I ride off into the blazing sunset

Disappearing in darkness afterward until discovery dispels it

I'm blessed by the evening breeze; the moon, emergent, silvers things

Scattering every shadow but mine, the night deciding my species

I was given a name, developed a voice, expanded the arsenal of my vocabulary

Nothing misspelled, spells pronounced carefully

Elements and ceremony, a balancing act erratic
'til I know what to call my lunatic magic

THINGS YOU CAN'T HAVE

Inner peace, all-encompassing contentment
Letting go without a trace of resentment

Kissing my mom's hand again, seeing her smile
Making Heaven on Earth last longer than a while

A dog whose lifespan is as long as they deserve
Falling in love and not getting hurt

A week without misspeaking
A year without feeling sick

Knowing what the creator's scheming:
How their OCD makes everything tic

Making your answer matter when your dad asks:
"Did I ever tell you the story…"

Warming up a sociopath's heart
Saddling up on meteors storming

These are all things you can't have
Things that won't happen or you can't do

But I'm aiming for all of them anyway
and sweetheart, so should you

GREY MATTER

You're sure you know
what forces I can marshal
What I'm a part of
or apart from
All I've ever been
or may yet be
Who I am
and who I'm not

Find my grey matter fresh then
Get my temper while it's hot

FRIENDLIEST DEMON

A thimble full of my spilled life blood

Ten seconds of a minute of my sentences served

The lowliest and friendliest demon I defeated

A hint of one secret gulped down for safekeeping

A wild stab at my knowledge which can't be proven

One day baring soul compared to my lifetime behooving

Any of these isolated is a minor tearing asunder

or a splintering into kindling if they dogpile together

So luck be with you and Heaven's holy light high-five you

If you mean to administer my attitude adjustment

Instead I might adjust yours

until it pops your fucking dials off

I'll work how I work

get rich off my naïve wish

bad actors in bad faith

won't knock me out of alignment

So tell the whole tri-state area

Something's wrong with my compass

But I trust my hellion trail

You're the specter I shouldn't have trusted

If you lack my lewd tastes

The next song might be different

What flavor, what sound

explains this schism's persistence

JACKALS ATTRACTED

The world was all sharp edges
I woke up every day half defeated
Predators and scavengers smelled blood:
Jackals attracted by my weakness

Now their most powerful pounce
won't bring me down:
I'm learning how to beat this

And you don't really remember me
You only remember my neediness

You don't really know me
I've got some brand new secrets

IT HURTS

It hurts but I can handle hurt

It hurts but I won't suffer

It hurts but if I'm active enough

the hurt gets lost in the shuffle

MURDEROUS

Take away
the murderous murmurs
Fold and store
the lolling loose tongues
In conniving skulls, sew them shut

Wake faith to spite
the malingerers motus operandi
Fortify and restore
the stomped on soul
Be on time arriving, make sure your blades cut

Unbury love
untangle it from opportunists
Befriend better nature
Don't revenge because you could
Singe and sage the loose ends, save our names in the book

Teach to touch without torture
dare without dying for it
Endless impenetrable deceptions
bid them backfire and detonate them
Call out the complicit, litigate a history of carnage brooked

TO REACH YOU

Came a time of unrest
Tamed some tigers I guess
But I couldn't reach the rest
Now the yard's a bloody mess

Found devices to reach you
Employed laptop and smartphone
Sent a beacon of the brain type
to remind you I ain't died

To you, yes I did
your absence says

The thought makes me shiver even in stillness
Before each perplexed, breathless step

Into what still remains with
Who still shows up
The same clouds every day
The same fervent prayer
until it's enough

GEMEINSCHAFT

Captive in a place devoid of quiet
Beating wings against a cage without bars
Every one of us might deny it
The hubris placing us here was ours
Mangled meanings we smooth out to analyze
Emoting in support groups, arguing over chores
Let's make our tangled lives mean more

IF

If you're looking for a reason to give up,
you'll eventually find one

If you're looking for transformative love,
remember you're God's fortunate daughter or son

If you need someone to bail you out,
people care more if you don't bring them down

If you know "verve" means movement,
show some and move it

If you get better, I'll say
I always hoped I knew it

If I know anything, it's that
ghosts never stop speaking

If you don't want to be one,
mine relentlessly for meaning

If nightfall finds you lonely,
treat yourself friendly

If day finds you rebounding,
treat the less lucky gently

If people don't understand you,
don't try too hard to understand why

If you understand you
smile big, don't be shy

If grief grabs you suddenly,
hold it close and mourn with it

If relief is unthinkable,
link with me, we'll think more of it

If that doesn't get you humming,
it'll never be for lack of trying

If you sit me down and say you'll listen,
it won't help if you're lying

If things can never be on the level,
it might all capsize into the sea

If you don't want me with you,
I don't want you with me

SORROW'S SONG

Brought out of shadow by a beacon
Touched and taught new depths of feeling
Chakras open and cards all laid out
to unveil purpose in the adept's doubt
Until our days are filled with praise
for both the sunbeam and the cloud
sorrow's song must be allowed and raised

PLANTING SEEDS IN A WARZONE

I can list comprehensively
good causes to fight for
but against who, in defense of who
obscures from hour to hour

The enemy is not quite invisible
but disconcertingly ephemeral
Trading places, choosing faces
to contort for a minute with malice
Then gone to leech another host
before I can retaliate

Well-equipped for battle
Just tired because
the war doesn't matter
Doesn't make a difference
The corrupt and dumb still reign

Planting seeds in a warzone
grows only bitter crops
So I promised myself I wouldn't
help them cultivate pain

Please do not be
another soldier of oppression
Your generals will not care for you
unless you fire blind

I don't want to bring myself
to pierce even a corrupted hide
So I may not stay to stop you

Not a single one of us
is absolved enough to die

STRAY SPARK

Made me your project without even asking

I keep quiet my endgame, nobody's beeswax

Big talk so wordy, lots to unpack

I'll survive just to piss off punks

Hide among God's gifts taken for junk

In day's dying light, night's lethal dark

My alchemy bleeds, ignites every stray spark

LOVE

LOVELESS

Football culture
Boring
Blaring
A deafening blandness
assaulting the senses

I don't come here
out of love for the sport

Beer hat culture
Temptation of temperance
Escaping
Causing
and making love to
our hopelessness

I could go anywhere
to fondle my despair

What is it
do you think
that brings me
day after day

Just guess
It's easy

You're right if
you guessed the name
you used
when we made introductions
I've loved the sound of it
ever since
though it can't quite
do you justice

You're a soul-stirring song
even during shitstorms
Love me or
let me be loveless

ANTE UP

Secrets stowed for all our safekeeping
Even when luck's a bitch, you can be sure that it's his

He quit smoking like he said, you just smell his smoke show
Ante up, take a gulp, you can't always run from risk

He loans you his coat, he looks you in the eye
Auburn flashing red, a jawline for miles

It's so big on you, he's 6'5, a pillar of power
He makes short work of work, pleasures all hours

The pleasure's all time's, the pleasure's all yours
Lean in for a whisper, be surprised what you get

The measure of the man is mad long, multifaceted
Tap him for your roster, your whole squad in his debt

LET'S NOT FIGHT

Another year older without getting colder
Still crying and laughing
Defending, attacking
in the heat of some impassioned cause
My sleeve embroidered with
my heartfelt flaws

Another year longer, weaker and stronger
Still capsizing and launching
Pretending, accepting
in the aftermath of some impossible love
My dreams embattled by
bigotry and drugs

There was a time that time passed slowly
Now it gallops to vanish
over cliffs and horizons
Around bends, right through happenstance
Leaving some things and stealing others
Leaving me wondering, showing me wonders

There was a time that time was my ally
Now most of the time it isn't
It demands and accuses
about goals and commitments
Some of which I accomplished
Most of which I didn't

Another year musing
there was a time for everything
Now I'm assuming
there's still time to make the most of things
Maybe I'm wrong but maybe I'm right
We're armored for war, but mi amor, let's not fight

KNOW THE DIFFERENCE

Damn this whole month
This calendar flicker
Damn you who loves me
but will not remember

Slow my December
A new year's redundant approach
Breeders spilling on my shoulder
Shoving me roughly, laughing and gabbing
So many of them
it renders my loneliness staggering

Tattooed under skin
A love's diamond image
Unwanted defense
of my diamond hard edges

False start and worse
Backwards progression
Too small for
my own shoes is how
they'd wish me
if I let them

Quench my boredom
The despair within it
insistent
I know both you and
how you script yourself
Knowing both
I know the difference

YOUR POWER

Where'd you slink off to, cool cat?
Where in what world are you
easing into your sunbathing wait
while I marvel still to feel
you paw my fevered cheek

I envision you but can't find you
Find you but can't feel you
You start to matter, then leave me to shatter

I shatter
and the breaking builds me

You know my secret language a little
You give old words new meaning

You serenade the freak in me
You smoke him out of hiding

Peace imploding
All my pieces imploring
Shyness I'm shorn of
begging and brazen
upon your permission
by your stray glance devoured
Flung on your floor
Floored by your power

I shouldn't stay
but I can't look away
Because you are serenity
and because you are shockwave

PLAY ON

You ride in on masked intent
On every plain at once
A chorus with a hook try as I might I've never shook
If I give up it's not abrupt
Man, just stop trying to get enough
I know everything we both did wrong and how much of it's
Not fit for song but there are moments here and there
That say "play on"
They say "play on"
So I hit repeat and I play on

Turn up the tune that's catchy
Tune out those I won't let catch me
All the while, in the physical realm,
In no hurry, you lie in wait
Powerful
Preternaturally calm
Singing to shifting fate
Bending again to give you your way

Everything that hears your serenade
Tilts with the music, irrevocably swayed

Do you know anything of the energies you cast
How they infiltrate my entirety
When your smile makes a room swoon
Or I'm lulled by your laugh

Not your problem, really
Not a problem at all
Fuck or attack, it's all my favorite track
So if you're playing me
Play on
Play on
With a warning that being
Weak for you has made me strong

If you're still listening, admit you like the song

NARROW ESCAPES

I imagine you with your feet up
Aloof about everything but your video game
Cheshire smiling while you click the combo
and tear right through the other guy

In the cramped shed you threaded wires to
from the house you either don't want to live in
or can't because your people withdrew kinship

They let you pirate their electricity
Not exactly an embrace
but a refusal to let you freeze

The prodigal never burnt out on the party
Faking change on your fashion forward odyssey
Do you forgive anyone ever
or are grudges cultivated as a matter of policy

I've forgiven you a great many things
and I can't forgive myself for it
because it doesn't feel like I'm doing it for me

That's what everyone says, isn't it?
Forgiving is for the wronged, not the one
who wielded a whole war's worth
of wrong against them

To me it feels like
another thankless favor I did you
absolving you without any
itemization of what for

What comforts of mine do I
not know you laced
You king of hidden things
You knave of narrow escapes

Will you ever forgive me
for knowing antidotes to
your pretty poisons
For discovering antivenom in
an assemblage of ordinary joys

Are you descending into revenging
to punish me for transcending

PAST MATTERING

I can't say for sure I'd notice
if you slipped in a lie

If your studded ear was gleaming
Caught right by the light

If your words were past mattering
If I could only hear your voice

I can't say for sure I'd believe in you
if I felt it were a choice

TRUE TO MYSELF

Here I am

I found me

Damn it's good to see me

I'm holding my own hand now

Losing me was too easy

I still love you like crazy

I'd still put you before me

But you disappeared on both of us

So I'm respecting your right to ignore me

I hope you answer yourself when you cry out

wondering what the hell happened

Even if you never miss me

I wish you every happiness

I still carry the torch

Still cradle the candle

So what

So fucking sue me

That's just me being true to myself

I didn't give up

You did

WE LINGERED

It's not really of our choosing, is it?
There was never a chance for us at all
I had mine and you had yours but
Not much ever felt like ours

I mean, the sex was a significant saving grace
Each other's bodies, we gave three and a half stars
We made fun of the same parts of movies,
so there's that,
and we had a few good talks
But we lingered leaps and bounds from
"let no one tear apart"

It's all relieved so easily
It won't survive
It isn't art

LOVE'S UNLIMITED FORM

Take this in to display in your museum
Do your hallways not sound empty
when your own footfalls try to fill them

Artifacts on loan
Never wanna give them back
Plaques inside of cases
engraved with: *all he had*

Soundtracks of your days
Creation's divided voice
Overlooked exhibits which
even you avoid

Cracking wax
dropping to the floor
Systematically dismantling
what history says you were

Love's unlimited form
in variations and permutations
Theories still untested
For lack of funding
and experimentation

Accusing glares preserved
in snapshots of
your species endangered
Sanctuary disturbed
by the rumble of many failures

Take this in to display in your museum
Do your mistakes not confuse you
all over when you repeat them

TRADING

Broke, no flow of green or gold
what I offer is visions for trading
and tricks of my trade
for honor bound assurance
if you need me just call
I'll come running for certain

A protester by my nature
A soldier in your service

NIGHTMARES OF YOU

I know where we're headed but not where I'm going
I know what you're doing but not where we'll end up

Long ago when creation started unfolding
Anything anywhere must have seemed like enough

Not long ago my heart was stolen
Now love just feels too easy to corrupt

I know what I mean but not how you'll take it
I know you're too mean to ever let me say it

Long ago you came over and shared my blankets
You talked me into touching you and then blamed me for it

Sometimes I have nightmares
of you eclipsing my moonlight

Sometimes I have dreams
that you'd help me fight

Every single person who hates our potential
Every solitary demon born of my solitary confinement

Every damn twist of fate like a blade stabbing deeper
Would you stem the flow or leave me for the reaper

VESSEL

It was barely perceptible
like it usually is
at first
Ran me down gently
You didn't have to move

So what now
This body
Granted mine
Granted yours

If this is my vessel
Why's it follow your pulse

REMINDING US

The anchor between my shoulder blades
weighs less since I met you
when I sneezed in line and you offered me
your hanky and your "bless you"

The glass that was half empty
overflows now, nothing can stop it
since you found something beautiful
in a stoner, bloodshot and sloppy

The mournful wind howling
no longer reminds me of missed opportunities
because the timing couldn't be better
for fortune to favor bravery

The hands that held themselves
are now clasped firmly in yours
investing with increasing intensity
No trace of buyer's remorse

The light so recently useless
above a porch no one visited
now beacons your way back to me
reminding us love can be innocent

LOVE SONGS PROMISE NOTHING

Love songs promise nothing
to those who didn't write them
You breeze in without intentions
Breeze out and don't inspire them

Still
I found ten in your skin tone
and your eyes got me thinking
of all my favorite albums

So
don't let me hear your laughter
Because then
I'd have to add new music
to my collection
Fly through a forest
of notebook paper

All so I'm not
alone with this
in a world
spinning indifferent

WAYS TO BLEED

I don't know why God had us meet
I just know why I want it to be
I can't be sure I'll ever get to be your good luck charm
But even when I'm what's risky, I try to keep you from harm

I'm not dressing these words up much
Just confessing I'm moved and I'm touched
Every moment of attention you show me eases a world of pain
Even the pain we dished out to one another
when my unpredictable seasons
tested the limits of your summer swagger

If I'd known it was something
that meant you couldn't be friends with me
When you told me your name I would have said
"Doesn't matter, I'm elderly"
But when 35 years yanked your illusions away
and shot you straight through your soul
You forget people don't already know

"This one hides" I thought of you then
"This one expects others to hide for him"
"Expects others to help him hide"
While you were misreading my body language
I was incorrectly assuming your type
Even though I was hiding too
Right in the middle of everyone
Hell, I'd feign brave with anyone
Pretending to be the man with all the right politics
and not a man fresh out of tricks

If you failed to acknowledge me
I resolved to rile up some unreason
If you didn't make mention that I exist too
I balled up all my belligerence
Let it rip with no regard for witnesses
Got so verbose your messages overflowed
And now I'm mad cos everyone knows
That I'm far too fucked up
To love anyone who isn't nuts
Which they'd have to be, to ride with me
even though I pay for everything

Wiled out in so many ways I shouldn't have
Investigated every impulse I shouldn't have
'til it was no wonder I couldn't ward off panic attacks
Head hung between my knees breathing into a paper bag
Which didn't for a moment disrupt your free flowing humblebrag

There's only one reason I should find you out
I don't know what it is yet, so I hope I find you home
I just know it exists, because your spirit stays all summer
even after you go ghost
I need some hows narrowed down, need to rule out some whys
Not that I still give a fuck except that when I care, that shit's for life
And outrage is no antidote, I remind myself too late all the time

So shake my hand, hug me goodbye, say "hello, bro" or "go"
Offer explanation or act easily scared
Haul off and hit me with your fist or that blue-green glare
that makes me want to grab you by the throat
Show you who I am, and why you better take note
If I gotta, I'll get in your face to attain some fucking grace

To get us to where we both have enough info to know
If everyone you are is really done with all of me
There's lessons still to learn is all
There are still some ways to bleed

ANOTHER SPIN

Sunlight, lush green leaves
say why even worry
what will happen will happen
in its own time and season

My fight, your mean streak
both weigh in spewing fury
I'm snapping, you're snapping
our crimes getting brazen

Do you even need to sleep
as much as you need something for another spin
I'll take something to spin me the other way

Doesn't always work the way it should
Try as I might
I just can't relax on Vicodin

Barely time to beseech
forgiveness between sinning sprees
I offend, I sharpen arguments
Sounding off with a litany of fault
most of it yours
based on circumstantial evidence

Money's not as nice as the things that have no price
If you love it so much
how come you're not smiling with your eyes

What comes easy isn't always what's wise
Expectations are mostly just things to defy

If I ever don't grant you
Something you want
It's because you're demanding
Something that haunts

Once you've spent everything you just can't take with you
I hope you still have what you came with
that no one can give you

HAIKUS ABOUT BEING AT YOUR MERCY

Damn, you're looking fine
You're hurting me just for spite
Can't say I'm surprised

*

I know I love you
I don't know if you love me
Begging cruel fate "please"

*

You're so far away
You used to follow closer
Bring back yesterday

*

Hardest thing to say
"Without you, I'm not ok"
Instead I'll save face

*

Wanna know the truth?
You look my way, I'm locked
No turning it off

*

Breeders get worked up
policing orientation.
Haven't you had enough?

*

I keep editing
every poem about you
divining your truth

*

Remember the time
you spent the night for months
although you're not mine

*

Spent so much money
on efforts to spoil you
you're still so damn cool

*

"I'm a casual dude"
you claim despite evidence
We pretend it's true

COSMIC FEVER

Breathing against each other
Beside ourselves beneath the covers
Caught up in cosmic fever as hands meandered
He told me stories and asked me questions
and stole my answers with famished kisses

We tripped the wire
We held the grenade
Exploded together
Exploded again

I've never forgotten
I've found no bigger bang
I explode alone remembering
Knowing no better way

ALL OF THE ABOVE

What if the real risk lies in playing it safe
What if we fear what we might give up
so much we never know what we'd gain
What if the one who would treat us like gold
is someone we toss aside cheaply
What if we took one leap of faith
and our reward was constant
for facing a fear that was momentary
What if I can still hear your verse and your chorus
even when you insist there's no music playing
What if we're art, unexamined, disregarded
What if we fight each other
so we don't have to fight for anything
What if the sum of your pleasure
thus far in your life
is a shadow, an echo, static
What if I can bring you bliss beyond measure
A spectrum unlimited, a crescendo electric
What if we run when we should chase
What if we hide when we should seek
What if we're done
when we should be just beginning
What if you won't listen, what if I won't speak
What if we falter at every fault in each other
with no sense of what we could have perfected
What if it scares you that I'd never hurt you
What if you hurt us both because you're offended
What if you do what you must just to be accepted
'til there's no you that you left unrejected
What if I never ask you any of this

because I already know all these answers
What if you stop making me ask you
What if this time, you surprise me
and that's what makes this time different
What if we both disarm our usual defenses
What if we make each other exceptions
What if I don't care how you label yourself
What if you don't care
how bad bigots get scared by our existence
What if it's sex, what if it's love,
What if it's revelation or all of the above

GRAVITY

All I am
All felt, fought or seen
Comes back to embers
ridges, storms and seas
None of which
Retain your constant gleam
Even though you're nothing like you seem

All my life, burning and scraping
Staring into stormfronts
Going to tempt the undertow
Even when it's unwise to spark or to swim
Despairing stillness that pursues
Everywhere I go

Bright line dividing
The time since we entangled
From everything before, discarded on your shore
All I was
All hidden, hyped or handed
All erased, all undone
Once your gravity grabbed me
Kinda can't complain
The stubborn heart will always
Find its way to celebration
But this love affair's not even there
Just reflexive contemplation of a hyper imagination

LOVE THEM AND ADMIT IT

I assume that I can't do it
That loving it assures I'll lose it
Maybe it doesn't
My entire past wasn't
a curse to identify
To be freed of
or equalize
Maybe the scales are balanced
I can walk the streets
and love them
and admit it on the crosswalks
and kiss you in the rainfall
and when I get you home
I can dry you off
and love you regardless
of net gain or net loss
Maybe you mattering to me
won't drain my batteries
but just rev the verse engine
Reverse over the curse
I created when I
should've been writing
Should've been loving
and knowing that's exactly
what I was doing
What was happening
Miraculously
on every street
where free men sleep
Fitfully or contentedly
Happy where they stay
or needing a better day
Daring loud or dying out
Dreaming either way

THIS NEED

Stranded in place except for altered states
Bringing our tension to higher planes

Lets me see you and I through different eyes
Both of us kind of crazy, both somewhat sane
Both of us darkened by idealism's demise

We keep fighting each other when we're both going under
I try sometimes to lift your head from the water
because despite my best efforts
I care whether or not you breathe

We keep lying to each other and we'll tear truth asunder
Only aggression's honest, I should fight you smarter
I pull my punches when we tussle and
you hit me even harder
Because despite my best efforts
you have this need for me to bleed

I have this need to change your mind about that
Writing about you again as if words will bring you back
As if the right verbiage will ring longer
Ring louder
Than you calling me the problem
and calling yourself the power

I have this need to prove you wrong
To hear you admit it
This need to love you and good reason to fear it

I have this unyielding need
and it co-opts every poem
This blistering need
Heavy heart caught in its undertow
Heavy head I try not to hang low

PRECIPICE
(In memory of Oz, 2007 – 2023)

It's not that I'll ever
for a second consider you gone
I feel your amiable presence
around bends in your old ambling trail
Glimpse your astral body in
the ricochet of sunbeams laughing;
Your smile wide with soul
on your measured, mayor-like stroll

It's just that the last hug wasn't labeled as such
I didn't know the chicken nugget split down the middle
with your sister would be your very last half a nugget ever

I didn't predict the last time I walked you
would be our last time side by side and both alive

I did predict you'd walk beside me still
and my boy, I was right, because now you're love alight

Still my center is shocked trying to process the memory
of reaching down to pick you up and finding only
the heaviness of a body
The sudden heartrend on such a scale
that the pumping red muscle fluttered
like some precarious bird in my chest
Lame winged, teetering on a precipice

> I held you, tried willing your warmth back
> I couldn't get it to work, but I seemed to freeze
> Steadied myself against the onrushing
> walls of blind grief
>
> I stumbled numbly
> I am still stumbling
>
> What fell was everything
> What falls is everything

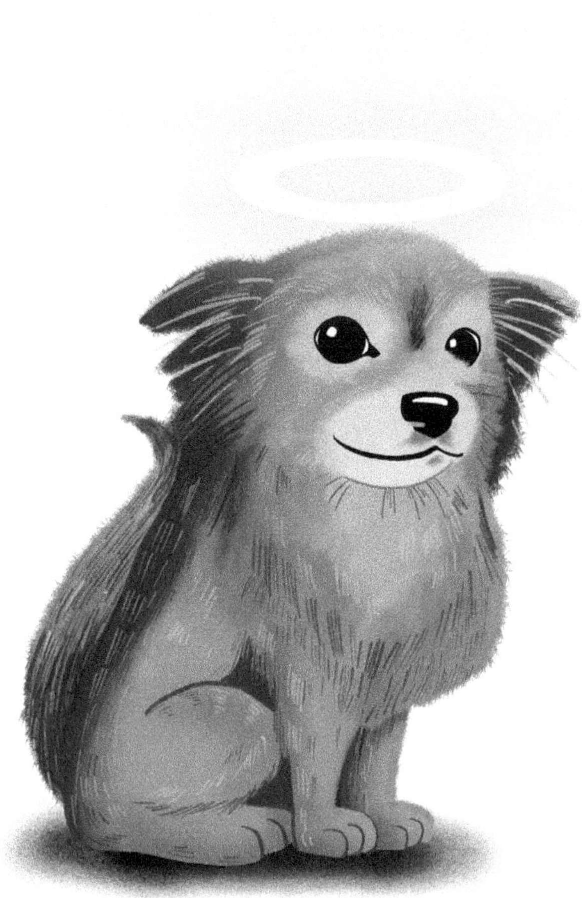

ABOUT ATMOSPHERE PRESS

Founded in 2015, Atmosphere Press was built on the principles of Honesty, Transparency, Professionalism, Kindness, and Making Your Book Awesome. As an ethical and author-friendly hybrid press, we stay true to that founding mission today.

If you're a reader, enter our giveaway for a free book here:

SCAN TO ENTER
BOOK GIVEAWAY

If you're a writer, submit your manuscript for consideration here:

SCAN TO SUBMIT
MANUSCRIPT

And always feel free to visit Atmosphere Press and our authors online at atmospherepress.com. See you there soon!

ABOUT THE AUTHOR

TRAVIS HUPP lives in the Shenandoah Valley of Virginia, where guys like him sometimes have to make their own fun. *Sin and I* is his second book. His first, *Faster, Annihilators!*, is also available wherever books are sold.

Milton Keynes UK
Ingram Content Group UK Ltd.
UKHW021944270524
443198UK00011B/114/J